ETHEL ARCHER

THE WHIRLPOOL

WITH AN INTRODUCTION BY
ALEISTER CROWLEY

AND AN INTRODUCTORY SONNET BY
VICTOR B. NEUBURG

THIS IS A SNUGGLY BOOK

This edition Copyright © 2023 by Snuggly Books.

ISBN: 978-1-64525-133-0

This Snuggly Books Edition is an unabridged, slightly amended version of that which was pubished by Wieland and Co. in 1911.

THE WHIRLPOOL

ETHEL ARCHER (1885-1962), the daughter of a clergyman, was born in Sussex, and expelled from school at the age of fourteen for asking questions in Scripture class. In 1908 she married the aspiring artist Eugene Wieland, and lived with him in West London. The couple made the acquaintance of Aleister Crowley, joined his A∴A∴ magical organization, and set up a publishing company called Wieland and Co., to publish Crowley's periodical *The Equinox*, as well as other texts, including Archer's first poetry collection *The Whirlpool* (1911). She published two other books, *Phantasy and Other Poems* (1930) and the occult novel *The Hieroglyph* (1932).

ALEISTER CROWLEY (1875-1947), was one of the pre-eminent English occultists, as well as a prolific writer and publisher. Among the vast number of his publications, was the poetry collection *Clouds without Water* (1909), and the novel *The Diary of a Drug Fiend* (1922).

VICTOR BENJAMIN NEUBURG (1883-1940) was an English poet who became closely aligned with Aleister Crowley, who initiated him into his magical organization the A∴A∴, and would later say that Neuburg "produced some of the finest poetry of which the English language can boast."

CONTENTS

Introduction / 7
Dedication / 9
To E. A. / 11

The Dreamer / 17
To a Skull amongst the Roses / 21
To Lilith / 25
The Song Virginal / 29
Midsummer Morn / 33
The Wisdom of Folly / 37
The Feloon Flower / 41
The Maelstrom / 47
To V. B. N. / 51
Storm and Sunrise / 55
The Felons' Fortress / 59
Reverie / 63
The Snow-Queen / 67
Sunrise and Sunset / 73
Lines to "The Great High Priest of
    Elemental Passion" / 77
Midsummer Eve / 83
Sleep / 87
Song to Leila / 91

INTRODUCTION

IN the waste horror of the Bralduh Nala, just before it opens out into the valley of Askole, is the hot spring. A perfect circle; water like a beryl, crowned with light sulphurous steam, the wall a mound like the breast of a woman of purest white, an efflorescence.

It is the hell of sterile passion glowing in the heart of the hell of desolation.

So also is this book. The intricacy of faery pattern which the witch weaves is the flowered marble. We find such rime-webs as abaaab—babbba and AaBCcAaBCcAaBC and bAbAcBcBACDADA, more exquisite than all the arabesques of the Alhambra.

The limpidity of thought and expression alike is the aquamarine of the pool: "Like foam-flowers falling from the breasts of Sleep their Lotus-kiss is," languid as Sappho writhing to the breeze of Leucadia, under a rain of roseleaves.

The hot angry famine and pestilence of the soul is the sulphur of the spring and the poisonous mist that plays upon it. "Come, Love, nor list to tired dreams that twist thy lithe long limbs in fierce abandonment," fierce as Pasiphae in Edmond d'Haraucourt's secret masterpiece; all the joyous torture of the damned in a phrase.

Dear lady, when this flask of perfume comes from the bookseller, you shall tire your hair, and paint your face, and gild your nails; you shall anoint yourself with the witch-ointment, and in the rosy twilight touch with a flame the pastilles of musk and ambergris. Then you lie upon the leopard's skin before the fire of sandalwood and read, and read.

And you shall know strange devils; even, it may be, strange gods.

ALEISTER CROWLEY.

DEDICATION

ALL that the Gods have taught Man through the gentle breath of the ages is discernment by comparison! God gave Light that we could judge the depths of Eternal Night; Love that we could know of Hate; Hell that we could know the joys of Heaven.

Comparison is only contrast. Happy contrasts form the happiness of Life.

Therefore from the blackness of my own Soul do I dedicate this volume to that secluded little world of white which gathers round

"THE EQUINOX"

There, if sin is not unknown, *Sin itself* cannot exist. There, if they cannot raise Man and place him on the knees of the Gods, they bring the Gods to Man.

O communicants of Nuit, Thoth, and Hathor, accept these poems, if only to form a contrast to your own illuminating genius!

Swathed in swart shrouds of the Silence of Hell,
Mid darkness too utter for thought to tell,
 I wander despairing; ALONE I dwell,—
Mere blackness burst from a clod.
Born of blind gloom ere the making of God,
As the sightless corpses beneath the sod.

Am I marked with a primal deadly curse?
Short shrift, my brothers, for better or worse
I smile,—and the horrible farce rehearse;
And goodness masquerade still.
Flanked by the germs of invidious ill
Since aught must be evil I do, or will.

E. A.

TO E. A.

The radiance of darkness, and the surge
    Of waves of blackness, and the lucent veil
    Of violet light, compounded with the pale
Red light of passion, here commingled urge
The spirit to adoration: on the verge
    Trembles a fiery Soul! Hail! Hail! oh, Hail!
    Thou lyric laughter of the enfranchised Male,
Thou fury of the eternal Woman's dirge!

Ah! Lesbos! let thy waves receive once more
    This soul tormented, striving still to gain
The land of laughter, and the hungry shore!
    Ah! Sappho! thou art born on earth again!
Call to thy lover till the fiends adore
    Thy soul, and the angels cry aloud for pain!

V. B. N.

THE WHIRLPOOL

THE DREAMER

To Bunco

IN the grey dim Dawn where the Souls Unborn
May look on the Things to Be;
A tremulous Shade, a Thing Unmade,
Stood Lost by the silent Sea;
And shuddering fought the o'erwhelming thought
Of Its own Identity.

Is the frenzied form that derides the storm
A ghost of the days to Be?
And the restless wave but the troubled grave
Of Its own dread Imagery?
Or merely a wraith cast up without faith
From the jaws of a Phantom Sea?

To his Love Unborn in that grey dim Dawn
Did the Shade of the Dreamer flee;
Nor marked he the Flood where the Vision had stood
Which mocks for Eternity.
For the Soul he would wed was the Hope that had fled
In the battle with Destiny.

TO A SKULL AMONGST THE ROSES

WITHIN her wanton's lap where Summer showers
    Roses, red, riotous as early Spring,
  Her golden glory faint and blossoming
With more than mortal beauty, magic hours
Faint with the fragrance of a thousand flowers
    Steeped in the soul of Music—silencing
    All other sound than that which Sleep may bring
To breathing Beauty;—there the Death's-Head glowers!
    Yea! Death grins charnel-wise! His jaws half ope,
    Laugh at that lure, the shining silken rope
Vanity fashions. 'Cross the sockets deep
Her web she weaveth, that no man may peep
    Further in quest of Knowledge than the scope
Of Life's dimensions, so—the end is—Sleep.

Yea! Sleep for all! And how shall one foretell
The Dream's awakening! Answer! Is it well
    All ye who slumber silent in the dark
    Dead halls of Hela! Do ye wake to mark
Despair's long journey through the deaf'ning swell

Of lost Endeavour? Formless shapes embark
   Strange foes to capture? Or, remain ye stark
To dust returning? Say! O Sentinel!
   Ye answer not! Nor would ye an ye could,
   Great Uninvited One, whose jaws have stood
For all time open, and whose orbs are filled
With strange blind knowledge, that has ever stilled
   Those who have sought it, and have seeking viewed
What lies beyond, too late! For so ye willed.

Yea! Smile on ever! Hold thy secret yet,
   Seeing full well that no man shall return
   To wrest it from thee! Let the roses burn
In sweet confusion, and the winds forget
All things save passion and the faint regret
   That follows closest joy. And whilst we yearn
   For that we trow not, but would ever learn
More and yet more of Know! We shall not fret!
   Warm glows the West,—and in that ruby fire
   Red roses burn sweet incense to the pyre
Of fallen Day. Pure flaming hearts obsessed
By perfumed passion-subtly manifest
   As songs that stir that soul-vibrating lyre,
Whose music is the deep Sea's heart at rest!

TO LILITH!

MOTHER of Evil and Sin yet to be
Fount of Iniquity deep as the sea,
Fairer than mortals, than mortals more free,
Mother of Wickedness, hearken to me!

When first I came to thee tempted by fame,
Lover of madness, yet dreading the same,
Almost I feared thee, fierce yet tame.
Love has now lit an unquenchable flame.

Now that I love thee and prize what I love,
Nothing can harm me from Hell or Above,
For I am fallen! What depth *thou* canst prove!
Lost through Eternity ever I rove!

How shall I picture thee—how shall begin?
Lovely and Evil One nurtured in Sin!
Veiling those mystic eyes all thoughts within,
Smiling yet sorrowful, watching earth spin!

Form white as glittering foam toss'd by the sea,
Hair like the dusky shades clasped round thy knee,
Limbs of a wondrous grace, rare symmetry,
Shaped from a mould God broke since forming thee.

What is iniquity? What but a name!
Since I have followed thee naught is the same.
Love knows no barrier, Love knows no shame—
All is enveloped in rose-coloured flame!

So whilst the years extend, exiled I roam,
Spouse of the faithless wind seeking a home,
Hot as the arid wastes, light as the foam
Serpent-like writhing to Heaven's blue dome.

THE SONG VIRGINAL

To the Great One of the Night of Time

SAID I a rose? More should I liken Thee
    Unto the heavy-scented Lotus-flower,
Blooming in isles amid th' enchanted sea,
    Diffusing for one glad and transient hour,
    Perfumes of strange intoxicating power,
That chain the senses but awhile so free.

I am a dreamer—and in dreamy mood,
    All lovingly I linger at thy side,
My senses maddened by the glorious food
    Of thy near presence; whilst a fiery tide
    Of sweet and wild desire as yet untried,
Surges me through, nor soon may be withstood.

And thou art by me,—thy all-glorious form
    Of warm and radiant beauty, serpent grace,
Thrills to the touch of mine, till midst a storm
    Of maddening kisses we are face to face,
    And thou art quivering in my strong embrace,
Consumed by fiery passion pulsing-warm.

Thy heavy perfumed tresses clasp me round,
    Like to the tendrils of the early vine.
Thy snaky limbs in sensuous coils are wound,
    And like Medusa's dreaded locks they twine
    About me-till I nearer thee incline,
Nearer and nearer, and in joy surround.

I love thy warm white body, magic hands,
    That hold me for a while from dark despair.
I love thee, child-wife born in other lands,
    Clothèd in naught but thine own heavy hair,
    Mysterious, godlike, wonderfully fair,
And subject only to Divine commands.

I love thee! Spirit-body, mind and Soul,
    In sadness, gladness, madness, love thee still,
I love thee as one great mysterious Whole
    Which every void in my sense can fill,
    Thy voice, far sweeter than the blackbird's trill,
Thy myriad glances, fearless of control!

O come! My fair enchanting Lotus-flower
    Bear me across the opal-tinted sea.
Subdue me with thy wondrous weak'ning power,
    Siren that tell'st of sweet felicity,
    And I renounce all earthy destiny,
All that the gods may give me for a dower,
All! All! To be with thee, one brief mad hour.

MIDSUMMER MORN

To Nina Stainthorpe

WARILY the watchful shadows guard alone, the
            ambush'd green,
Till a whisper faintly dawning, fills the fragrant air of
      morning
Like a vague unuttered warning, to a host of
      Things Unseen.
Then the dew-drops glance and glisten on the leaves
      the fairies christen,
Whilst the still air strives to listen to their laughter
      sweet and keen.

From the silent shores of Midnight hath the dancing
      Day withdrawn,
And I long to tread the measure of her never-tiring
      pleasure,
Such as men and maids did treasure ere the troubled
      Fates were born;
And with soul but newly saddened, I would seek the
      joys that gladden'd,
And the many songs that madden'd all the minstrels
      of the morn.

But in vain from dusk to dawning, once the wondrous quest begun,
Do I plead with love unspoken, for the fragile fairy token
That shall bear my spirit broken, to the Lands beyond the Sun.
Yet when Hope herself seems lying, I may find it still undying,
In some Land, with Sleep slow-sighing, where our deeds and dreams are one.

THE WISDOM OF FOLLY

FOLLY, child of the fairies born in June,
　Her sweet bells jingling to a joyous tune,
Sought the dark depths of Knowledge. By the pool
She lay disrobed, and in the waters cool
Saw *still* her own reflection. Wearied soon,
Deeper she sought to fathom and to school
Her idle thoughts to Wisdom; so to rule
The world by Folly,—from sad cares immune!

A peacock's feather (late her sceptre gay)
Smiling she fashions as a rod to play
At fishing. For the stagnant pool is deep,
And Folly shudders at the things which creep
Below the surface; where pale lilies sway,—
Frail, starlike blossoms, wrapt in soulless Sleep.

THE FELON FLOWER

(A RHAPSODY)

AS the sighing of souls that are waiting the close
of the light,
As the passionate kissings of Love in the Forest of
Night,
As the swish of the wavelets that beat on a cavernless
shore,
Or the cry of the sea-mew that echoes a moment or
more,
So the voice of thy spirit soft-calling my soul in its
flight.

As the breath of the wind that is borne from the island
of Love,
As the swift-moving cloudlets that sail in the heaven
above,
As the warmth of the sunlight that breaks on the
shimmering sea,
And the sweetness that lurks in the sting of the
honey-fed bee,
So the joy of thy kiss, the dread offspring of serpent
and dove.

As the trail of the fiery lightnings that gleam in the dark,
As the light from the measureless Bow of the sevenfold Arc,
    As the fires which glance o'er the face of the treacherous deep,
    When none but the furies may rest, and the nereids weep,
So thy meteor eyes, brightest sirens alluring Love's barque.

When hid in the wonderful maze of thy whispering hair,
Alone with the shadows and thee, and away from the glare
    Of the burning and pitiless day, and the pitiless light,
    Thee only beside me, above me the mystical night,
No dream so created in darkness was ever more fair.

For then was thy touch as the light of a life-giving fire,
Which kindles, and scorches, and burns, with unsated desire,
    Thy breath the warm essence of myrtle, the fragrance of pine,
    The languorous smoke of a temple obscene yet divine,
Which gladdens the soul of a god in his passionate ire.

So silent those nights, I could fancy the uttermost
    deep
Engulfed us for ever,—for ever in silence to keep
  The tale of our wooing: till sweetly the murderous
    hours
    Had lulled us to rest; and the magical poison of
      flowers
Had stolen our brains, and our eyelids were heavy
    with sleep.

Ah love! They are banished, yet not so the strength
    of the spell
Which holds both our beings in bondage, a bondage
    so fell
  That even the angels above cannot alter its power;
  It lives in the memory yet of one passionate hour,
When from the dark bosom of Hell sprang a fair
    felon flower.

THE MAELSTROM

BEYOND that outer space which bounds the blue,
Beyond the confines of the furthest star,
Beyond all thought and sight, where comets bar the
    light,
But myriad motes the sunlight filters through!
Vaster than Time or Space, madly the planets race,
From ever widening circles drawn afar
As drifting spar,
Down to the whirling centre: there anew
To be cast forth, till haply lost to view
In That One Eye; which is the vortex.

Narrow the circles to resurging fire!
Stars battle blindly in that dim abyss.
See in the whirling tide, as one vast suicide,
Creation stagger! Yet the one desire,
Ever insatiate, must darkly gravitate
To that deep centre, till it comes to this:
Failing, we miss.
Missing, by that same failure we acquire
One chance the more,—so vainly we aspire
To gain our final goal,—perfection.

So far is comprehended. But one Eye
Of the All-Seeing holds our Universe.
Great though to Man the Storm, 'tis but a shadow-
    form
Slow-passing in that centre. How descry
Of that deep Eye, the Soul, the structure of the Whole,
The meaning of the Maelstrom, or that terse
Tremendous curse
By some called Destiny! The Eternal "Why?"
Mayhap is answered when Infinity
Becomes at last the Finite, and the End.

TO V. B. N.

WHAT silent shadow stirs the sentient air?
    Like some dim-whirling flame-flower from
  the Loom
Of Darkness; swifter circling 'mid the gloom
Of incense-laden shadows, to the air
Of softly chanted mantrams; till the prayer
  So oft-repeated fills the sombre room
  With magic mighty as the dusky plume
Of the Concealèd One, by whom we swear!

Victor! Twice Victor! By thy golden lays
Of many-moulded music, hear our praise!
  Accept our homage, whilst our spirit whirls
  With thine: in fiercest ecstasy unfurls
New glory ever,—till the vision slays
  Itself, of its own beauty, Passion's pearls.

STORM AND SUNRISE

AS a bird of sable plumage
Rising from a stormy ocean,
Sweeps the Night across the hilltops.
Ruffled are his shining feathers,
All his wings are dashed with water,
Drops which falling dull earth's torches,
Drown the stars in all their glory.
Then the pale-faced moon in terror,
Draws a veil across her features,
Bows her weeping head in silence,
Praying for the stars her children.
But the Night recks naught of sorrow,
Scornfully he rushes onward,
Shakes anew his gloomy pinions,
While his yellow eyes dart lightning.
From his cave beneath the mountains
Warily the Sun-god watches,
Shakes his crested head in anger,
Fixes flaming eyes upon him;
Yet the Night draws on undaunted.
Mocks the Sun-god in his fortress,

Cries: "O wherefore hid'st thou, Sun-god?
Fearest thou to meet thine equal?"
Then in great and awful anger
Flashing from his cave, the Sun-god
Bursts upon him in his fury,
Shoots him with a golden arrow.
And the Night in sinking downward
Splashes with his blood the Sun-god,
Dyes his yellow locks with crimson,
Stains the snow upon the hilltops.
Then the mortals in the valley
Laugh, and cry: "Behold the Sun-god!
See him flaming on the mountains,
See the Night our foeman burning,
Praise the Sun-god in his triumph!"

THE FELONS' FORTRESS

To George Raffalovich

MAIMED shadows move athwart the murky air,
    Pale, prayer-deluded phantoms, that the gloom
  Delights to cherish—as the hemlocked tomb,
The corpse of one whose life was scarce more fair
Than that of the grim ghouls who laid him there,
    Stripped of all covering till the Day of Doom.
    Gaunt as the carrion where the gallows loom,
Unhallowed Imagery of Man's Despair!

As night-moths flutter round the taper's head,
As vampires clamour o'er the smitten dead,
    So madly whirls the wind. The Midnight hour
    Is fraught with fears more gruesome than yon tower,
Where sin-gorged souls on curdling crimes have fed;
    The deep moat shuddering at the armed hordes' power.

REVERIE

WHEN Night unbinds her shadowy hair
    And starlight glimmers o'er the wave,
And grey old Neptune seeks his lair
    Within some coral-columned cave,
While dreaded Darkness silent stalks
    Where'er the Storm-fiends maddest rage,
Unfettered, the dim Spectre walks,
    The memory of a vanished age!

When sweet-browed Solitude reveals
    The April-radiance of her face,
And o'er the West the crimson steals
    In many a varied form of grace,
Upon the whispering wind is borne
    Soft music, from a world at rest,
And rustling garments sweep the corn
    Or stir the foaming billow's crest.

But when Aurora softly shakes
    Her golden tresses bathed in dew;
And o'er the East the sunlight breaks

In spear-like rays of sparkling hue,
Upon the mirrored waves is cast
　An image, that to Death is wed,
Then fades,—a shadowy form has past—
　The harrowing dream of hopes long dead.

THE SNOW QUEEN

(A DREAM)

I

I LOOKED,—and in the North a mountain stood,
   Its rugged sides outlined the wintry sky,
Around it and above, a silv'ry flood
   Shone soft and luminously from on high.

II

Upon the distant summit was a throne,
   Formed by fantastic fancy, ever new,
Whereon 'mid wreaths and diamonds widely strown
   The fairest of all mortals met my view.

III

Of mortals—if fair Nature, wayward child,
   Breaking the ties which bound her to this earth,
Should, 'midst the glories of another sphere
   To semi-mortal give a wondrous birth.

IV

The moon-beams kissed her pale celestial brow,
  Making a halo round her stately head,
Whilst high above the pure untrodden snow
  Towered gigantic, one huge pyramid.

V

Within her queenly hand a sceptre lay
  That pointed o'er the desert wastes afar,
As she, the lawful sovereign, held her sway,
  Like to the sweet and radiant evening star.

VI

Then o'er the distant hill tops, with the dawn
  Came there the winged messenger of Love,
And rosy glowed his pinions in the morn,
  As touched by Iris from the realms above.

VII

With undulating motion, like the breeze
  That fanned the rippling locks from off his brow,
He softly floated o'er the frozen seas,
  And lighted on the pure unspotted snow.

VIII

As if to greet him many a smiling flower
    Rose from the earth, the harbinger of spring,
Whilst from the clouds, poured down a golden shower
    Of mellow radiance from the Sunsteed's wing.

IX

The chaste and radiant goddess marked his flight,
    And from the depths of two soft starry eyes,
(Like a pale moonbeam on a misty night)
    Came there a smile of sweet and glad surprise!

X

She rose, and with her shapely arm entwined
    In his, towards sunset, furthest west they flew,
Warm Love and Purity to each inclined
    Rose higher, and did 'scape my mortal view.

XI

I from the arms of Morpheus then released,
    And tarrying 'twixt the fancy world and real,
My vision strangely beautiful now ceased,
    I marked the struggling sunbeams downward steal.

SUNRISE AND SUNSET

THE sun his golden Chariot drives afar,
  Chasing with lightning beams the morning star,
And gloom and shadows swiftly flee away
From him, the mighty monarch of the day.

All things on earth attest sweet summer's reign,
The hawthorn opes her fair white bud again,
Within each jewelled cup a dew-drop lies,
Its rainbow lustre borrowed from the skies.

The blackbird blithely carols forth his song,
Wafted the scented woodland all along,
And echoed in some joyful lover's heart,
Who with his blushing queen now walks apart.

On the still air breathes not a single word
Save when the cuckoo's mournful note is heard,
And sweet may-blossoms, lately fully blown,
Float softly, airily and lightly down.

Behind the distant hills he goes to rest,
Like some bright bird into a downy nest
Of crimson cloudlets, fringed with richest gold,
And purple-mantled waves with silv'ry fold.

Fair smiling Day has fled in rosy light,
Yielding a way to starry-kirtled Night,
Whose jewelled garment sweeps the vault of Heaven,
While myriad orbs look down, the darkness riven.

So, silence steals o'er the broad ocean deep,
And town and village soon are plunged in sleep,
Waiting Aurora in the flush of dawn,
To paint with fairest hues the coming morn.

LINES TO "THE GREAT HIGH PRIEST OF ELEMENTAL PASSION"

I

I DREAMED of a province of light,
Pulsating with passion, and free,
And my soul as a swallow took flight
From the shores of inscrutable night,
Till it stayed where the pale stars ignite
At the salt-laden kiss of the sea.
And caught in a cave of the free,
Where madness but masks new delight,
I was one with the soul of the sea,
As it surged with the passion of thee,
As it foamed with strange frenzy and glee—
Till the stars shuddered down at the sight.

II

And morn rose, a mist tinged with blood,
Her seal on our passion to set,
And a crimsoner foam flecked the flood,

As it lashed into fury, and stood
Like a stallion checked in the wood
By a stranger—ill-timed as ill-met!
Ah! Sweet was the struggle that set
The savage astir in the blood;
While we laughed for the love that had met
Naught so false, as that love to forget,
Naught too great, for that love to regret
While with passion the soul is imbued!

III

By the stars that ignite at the salt-laden kiss of the sea,
By the foam-frenzied fury that lashes the souls of the
    free,
By the gladness of madness that masks but a newer
    delight,
And the rapture of capture enfolded in arms of the
    night,
                                 I adore thee!

IV

By the silence enshrouded in darkness the depth of
    the tomb,
By the swift-footed phantoms which fathom the
    gardens of gloom,
By the coils and the toils of the serpent that sleeps in
    the brine,

And the charm and the calm of the ocean deep-souled
    and divine;
                              I adore thee!

V

By the mists of the mountain, where mingle the roses
    of morn,
By the leaves that the fairies have christened with
    laughters unborn,
By the gleam of the stream where immortal with
    mortal shall wed,
And the soul of the whole of creation by passion be
    fed;
                              I adore thee!

VI

By the songs of the forest which echo the chant of the
    stars,
By the red flaming planet which flashes the sigil of
    Mars,
By the wail of the gale as it lashes the trunks of the
    trees,
And the ghost of a host of dead phantoms are whirled
    on the breeze;
                              I adore thee!

VII

By the rapturous red of the roses, the ruin of rain,
By the poisonous passion of poppies, the perfume of
    pain,
By the dawn of the faun of desire, by the shudder of
    sleep,
And the swoon of the moon as she catches the cry
    of the deep;
                                   I adore thee!

MIDSUMMER EVE

To Osmond

FAINT shadows cross the shifting spears of light,
    Pale gold and amethyst or warmly white—
Till velvet shod, unseen, the wizard hours
Hold thus their elfin court amid the flowers,
    That wake to winged music of the night.
And silken sighs scarce stir the amorous bowers,
Where passioned Sleep his poppy-garland showers,
    In dreams which mock the hastening moments'
        flight.

Up soars the moon, and higher still and higher
    The dancers leap to catch some fairy fire
    To steal and prison in the glow-worm's tail,
For pixie torches should the starlight fail,
Reflecting gems which deck the elfin choir,
    Melting like snow-flakes at the daybreak pale.

SLEEP

To Emily

ALONG the silver pathways of the moon,
    (With lilies strewn to mark her passing hours)
        A mighty goddess strays.
Her rapt eyes gaze in calm undying swoon,
    Like stars in June that guard Earth's sleeping flowers,
        The guests of summer days.
Moving she plays some sweetly-slumbrous tune,
    As mothers croon; while faint aeolian showers,
        Her mist-hung garment sways.

And in her shadow chaste as starlit snows,
    A vestal goes; scattering sweet roses.
        Roses deep thorned and red,
Whose leaves are shed in perfumed dreams, where glows
    A world that blows and fairy-like discloses
        The fields that Flora fled.
And some are sped where dream brings that repose
    The thorn bestows—(where naught that is, reposes)—
        Goring the sleeper's head.

SONG

To Leila

COME, Love, awaken! O'er the wild salt sea,
Shadows strange-shapen whirl themselves and
    flee
As eddying mist, by storm-winds overtaken,
And sunbeams kissed the shafts all curled and shaken
In shuddering ecstasy!
Come, Love, nor list to tired dreams that twist
Thy lithe long limbs in fierce abandonment,
Awake, and learn of me the secret of the sea,
Whose meaning is the sum of all things blent
In fiercest harmony.

Soft winds are calling on the cloudy deep,
(Like foam-flowers falling from the breasts of Sleep
Their Lotus-kiss is). Such a world forestalling
Of wanton blisses, that the fear of palling
Makes e'en the Sirens weep.
Ah me! What serpent hisses from out those purple
    'bysses,
Far in the womb of the lone-lying sea.

She wakes! Nor dare he creep back to her soul,
    whence Sleep
Has torn aside the mist-hung drapery;
Too strange the way—and steep.

A PARTIAL LIST OF SNUGGLY BOOKS

ETHEL ARCHER *The Hieroglyph*
G. ALBERT AURIER *Elsewhere and Other Stories*
CHARLES BARBARA *My Lunatic Asylum*
S. HEZOLNRY BERTHOUD *Misanthropic Tales*
LÉON BLOY *The Tarantulas' Parlor and Other Unkind Tales*
ÉLÉMIR BOURGES *The Twilight of the Gods*
CYRIEL BUYSSE *The Aunts*
JAMES CHAMPAGNE *Harlem Smoke*
FÉLICIEN CHAMPSAUR *The Latin Orgy*
BRENDAN CONNELL *Metrophilias*
BRENDAN CONNELL *Unofficial History of Pi Wei*
BRENDAN CONNELL (editor)
    The Zinzolin Book of Occult fiction
RAFAELA CONTRERAS *The Turquoise Ring and Other Stories*
DANIEL CORRICK (editor)
    Ghosts and Robbers: An Anthology of German Gothic Fiction
ADOLFO COUVE *When I Think of My Missing Head*
QUENTIN S. CRISP *Aiaigasa*
LUCIE DELARUE-MARDRUS *The Last Siren and Other Stories*
LADY DILKE *The Outcast Spirit and Other Stories*
CATHERINE DOUSTEYSSIER-KHOZE
    The Beauty of the Death Cap
ÉDOUARD DUJARDIN *Hauntings*
BERIT ELLINGSEN *Now We Can See the Moon*
ERCKMANN-CHATRIAN *A Malediction*
ALPHONSE ESQUIROS *The Enchanted Castle*
ENRIQUE GÓMEZ CARRILLO *Sentimental Stories*
DELPHI FABRICE *Flowers of Ether*
DELPHI FABRICE *The Red Sorcerer*
DELPHI FABRICE *The Red Spider*
BENJAMIN GASTINEAU *The Reign of Satan*
EDMOND AND JULES DE GONCOURT *Manette Salomon*
REMY DE GOURMONT *From a Faraway Land*
REMY DE GOURMONT *Morose Vignettes*
GUIDO GOZZANO *Alcina and Other Stories*
GUSTAVE GUICHES *The Modesty of Sodom*
EDWARD HERON-ALLEN *The Complete Shorter Fiction*
EDWARD HERON-ALLEN *Three Ghost-Written Novels*

J.-K. HUYSMANS *The Crowds of Lourdes*
J.-K. HUYSMANS *Knapsacks*
COLIN INSOLE *Valerie and Other Stories*
JUSTIN ISIS *Pleasant Tales II*
JULES JANIN *The Dead Donkey and the Guillotined Woman*
GUSTAVE KAHN *The Mad King*
MARIE KRYSINSKA *The Path of Amour*
BERNARD LAZARE *The Mirror of Legends*
BERNARD LAZARE *The Torch-Bearers*
MAURICE LEVEL *The Shadow*
JEAN LORRAIN *Errant Vice*
JEAN LORRAIN *Fards and Poisons*
JEAN LORRAIN *Masks in the Tapestry*
JEAN LORRAIN *Monsieur de Bougrelon and Other Stories*
GEORGES DE LYS *An Idyll in Sodom*
GEORGES DE LYS *Penthesilea*
ARTHUR MACHEN *N*
ARTHUR MACHEN *Ornaments in Jade*
CAMILLE MAUCLAIR *The Frail Soul and Other Stories*
CATULLE MENDÈS *Bluebirds*
CATULLE MENDÈS *Mephistophela*
ÉPHRAÏM MIKHAËL *Halyartes and Other Poems in Prose*
LUIS DE MIRANDA *Who Killed the Poet?*
OCTAVE MIRBEAU *The 628-E8*
CHARLES MORICE *Babels, Balloons and Innocent Eyes*
GABRIEL MOUREY *Monada*
DAMIAN MURPHY *Daughters of Apostasy*
KRISTINE ONG MUSLIM *Butterfly Dream*
OSSIT *Ilse*
CHARLES NODIER *The King of Bohemia and His Seven Castles*
CHARLES NODIER *Outlaws and Sorrows*
HERSH DOVID NOMBERG *A Cheerful Soul and Other Stories*
PHILOTHÉE O'NEDDY *The Enchanted Ring*
GEORGES DE PEYREBRUNE *A Decadent Woman*
HÉLÈNE PICARD *Sabbat*
JEAN PRINTEMPS *Whimsical Tales*
JEREMY REED *When a Girl Loves a Girl*
ADOLPHE RETTÉ *Misty Thule*
JEAN RICHEPIN *The Bull-Man and the Grasshopper*
FREDERICK ROLFE (Baron Corvo) *Amico di Sandro*

JASON ROLFE *An Archive of Human Nonsense*
ARNAUD RYKNER *The Last Train*
LEOPOLD VON SACHER-MASOCH
  The Black Gondola and Other Stories
MARCEL SCHWOB *The Assassins and Other Stories*
MARCEL SCHWOB *Double Heart*
CHRISTIAN HEINRICH SPIESS *The Dwarf of Westerbourg*
BRIAN STABLEFORD (editor)
  Decadence and Symbolism: A Showcase Anthology
BRIAN STABLEFORD (editor) *The Snuggly Satyricon*
BRIAN STABLEFORD (editor) *The Snuggly Satanicon*
BRIAN STABLEFORD *Spirits of the Vasty Deep*
COUNT ERIC STENBOCK *The Shadow of Death*
COUNT ERIC STENBOCK *Studies of Death*
MONTAGUE SUMMERS *The Bride of Christ and Other Fictions*
MONTAGUE SUMMERS *Six Ghost Stories*
ALICE TÉLOT *The Inn of Tears*
GILBERT-AUGUSTIN THIERRY
  The Blonde Tress and The Mask
DOUGLAS THOMPSON *The Fallen West*
TOADHOUSE *Gone Fishing with Samy Rosenstock*
TOADHOUSE *Living and Dying in a Mind Field*
TOADHOUSE *What Makes the Wave Break?*
LÉO TRÉZENIK *The Confession of a Madman*
LÉO TRÉZENIK *Decadent Prose Pieces*
RUGGERO VASARI *Raun*
ILARIE VORONCA *The Confession of a False Soul*
ILARIE VORONCA *The Key to Reality*
JANE DE LA VAUDÈRE *The Demi-Sexes and The Androgynes*
JANE DE LA VAUDÈRE *The Double Star and Othe Occult Fantasies*
AUGUSTE VILLIERS DE L'ISLE-ADAM *Isis*
RENÉE VIVIEN AND HÉLÈNE DE ZUYLEN DE NYEVELT
  Faustina and Other Stories
RENÉE VIVIEN *Lilith's Legacy*
RENÉE VIVIEN *A Woman Appeared to Me*
ILARIE VORONCA *The Confession of a False Soul*
ILARIE VORONCA *The Key to Reality*
TERESA WILMS MONTT *In the Stillness of Marble*
TERESA WILMS MONTT *Sentimental Doubts*
KAREL VAN DE WOESTIJNE *The Dying Peasant*

www.ingramcontent.com/pod-product-compliance
Lightning Source LLC
Chambersburg PA
CBHW020544080526
44583CB00013B/991